The day the queen died

The day the queen died [and
other poems and some stories
about life that are very short and
not always sweet.]

Some of these poems and stories
have scenes that you might find
offensive. Readers are urged to
take care if they are sensitive to
rude language and scenes of a
sensitive nature.

For all victims of bullying and
other horrid acts. This book is a
tribute to you all.

A letter to DC

DC Leave me alone

Leave me the bleep alone.

Stop lying to me that Dominic's
dead

I wonder how you sleep in bed.

You lie so much your pants are
singed.

You are making me so unhinged.

I pinned you once against the
wall.

Now you tell folk I'm up the wall.

What have I ever done to you?

To make you act so cruel.

Did I annoy your precious auntie?

By breathing too loudly when I
was smaller.

The truth is you want someone to
blame

On me you try to bring terrible
shame

You can't cope that I am not lame

It's you that needs to carry the
blame.

The baby

I lie in bed, terrified and alone.

I hear my dad talking on the
phone.

The person on the other end

Says has she got a boyfriend?

I'm covered in blood and slime.

Pants ripped and no longer lime.

My grey trousers are still down

My face is wearing a terrified
frown.

I want my dad. I want my mum.

I don't want them to touch my
bum.

The doctor wears the white glove

The evil man stole my innocent
love

The kit is used. The truth is out.

And now I will scream and shout.

The baby is born. it is a boy.

His father broke me like a toy.

I look at him. He looks at me.

I see him in his eyes you see.

The boy must go. He must now
go.

DNA for the court. We already
know.

My mum j.

L will you put the dinner on? Right now. I know it's only half two and your group starts at three and doesn't finish until four, but I want my baked potatoes at four o clock on the dot.

Yes j.

L will you go to the shop for me?
Right now. I want four packets of
cheesy crisps and some chocolate.

Yes j.

L will you hurry up and serve the
dinner up. Its four-o clock and I
want my dinner.

Yes j. In a minute.

L will you take my plate into the
kitchen for me as I am too lazy to
walk five metres into the kitchen.

Yes j.

L will you get cakes out the shop
for me.

Yes J.

L I know your other zoom group is on in five minutes and you have just come back from the shop, but can you get bread as well as sugar. I want sugar for my cereal later.

Yes j.

While in zoom group meeting j shouts. L can you go to the shop and get me some beans as I just saw an advert for beans and want beans on toast now.

J I am in a zoom meeting.

It will only be five minutes.

Yes j.

L will you make beans on toast as
I can't work the easy-to-use oven
because I'm stupid.

Yes j.

L will you go to the wee shop for
me and get me……

It's eight o clock. Shop's shut.

Go to the Co-op and get me an ice
cream cone. In fact, get two.

Can I have one?

No. You are just to serve me.

I have been working all day and I
would like a cone.

I said no. I am too miserable to
buy you a cone.

Then I am not getting you two
cones or any cones. It's hot and I
am wanting a cone.

Do as you are told slave.

Puppy

I want a puppy

Oh it's so cute

I want a puppy

Ok I'll get you a puppy

Best mum ever

The creature

The fluffy stinky smelly ugly
creature

Rubbed itself around my mother

Get rid of that ugly creature she
cried

I saw the tears in the creature's
eyes.

I petted the creature he started to
purr

I lifted my hand. It was covered in
fur.

The creature was a cat and he sat
on the mat

I called him Bigfoot and he loved
me back

The cat called Bigfoot never loved
my mother.

He loved me more than he loved
his sisters and brother.

I loved him until the day he died.

He hugs me when he sees tears in
my eyes.

Love

Love is a thing that the blind can
see

The deaf can hear and we all can
touch.

So here he comes to marry me

We'll now cuddle on the couch.

Written in the time before I met
Chris

I just want a boyfriend.

I'm just a girl with hair of rust

I do not know if I can trust.

I trusted you. You let me down.

Like every single boy in town.

I've been trying to be happy
without one.

They say you don't need a man.

I feel like you just broke my heart
bone

Nothing can fix it. Not even
superglue can.

I just want a boyfriend.

I don't just want a friend.

I want someone to love who loves
me back.

Is that too much for me to ask
Jack.

My first kiss was a boy at college.

He did it as a dare for Colin.

At that point I just didn't care

Then he said yuck what an awful
dare

He put his tongue in my mouth

I felt a great delight

I was ready to ask him out that
day.

He pulled out and shouted no
way.

I just want a boyfriend.

I don't just want a friend

I want someone to love who loves
me back.

Is that too much for me to ask
Jack.

This pandemic made me realise.

I'm tired of being myself and
alone. Please...

...Help me find a decent man to
love.

Don't care if he's a tiger or a
dove.

I don't want to be

A 34-year-old virgin you see.

If he's good in bed, I wouldn't
know

To the church to get married we'll
go.

I just want a boyfriend.

I don't just want a friend.

I want someone to love who loves
me back.

Is that too much for me to ask
Jack.

I just want a boyfriend.

I don't just want a friend.

I want someone to love who loves
me back.

Is that too much for me to ask
Jack.

I just want a boyfriend.

I don't just want a friend.

I want someone to love who loves
me back.

Is that just too much for me to ask
Jack.

I take it that's just too much for
me to ask Jack.

I now have a boyfriend

He's more than a friend.

I got someone to love who loves
me back.

Our love is flowing down a chew
chew track.

The killing of a disabled baby.

The doctor starts the op, and my
mother falls asleep.

The cutting starts. I'm just a day
before I'm due.

My home is slashed into, and I see
the doctor's evil eyes.

He cuts apart my lifeline. I can't
breathe. I'm so afraid.

The doctor watches as I try to
breath in the water.

He doesn't help me. Because I am
disabled, he doesn't care.

I'm worthless to the doctor. I am
not allowed to live.

No birth certificate, no birthday
or No funeral. Just dumped in a
bag as medical waste.

To quote the doctor she must die.

I must have been dreaming of the
life I want to lead.

I'm sleeping in my warm and cozy
bed.

I heard my mother screaming and
I know she lost her head.

I heard the doctors saying that
they will make me dead.

To quote the doctor. she must
die.

I feel the brutal cuts as the
doctors slash my home in two.

I feel the hoover grab me as I
don't know what to do.

They cut my lifeline and I struggle
to breath a bit.

No hope no life no funeral. I never
even exist.

To quote the doctor she must die.

Ode to a Malteser. By Elizabeth
Mullen.

*Inspired by a Malteser I saw on a
bus journey I took on a Saturday
morning.*

I roll around on a glittery desert.

That's red and orange and shades
of blue.

I pause and rest. The sunlight hits
me.

I start to melt and fade away.

The sunshine goes. I roll some
more.

I touch a lady's trainer then
another.

The space is emptier than usual.

I'm trodden on. Misshapen now.

I feel the crush. My end is near.

What's left of me in the desert.

A mess of brown and golden husk.

Oh, chocolate cake

Oh, chocolate cake

Oh, chocolate cake

You are looking very yummy

Oh, chocolate cake

Oh, chocolate cake

You taste nice in my tummy

I Really Want to Meet the Singing
Kettle

I really want to meet the singing
kettle

I know they don't exist anymore

Artie, Cilla, Gary, Jane and the
others

And maybe peek in the editor's
door

I wish that I could have been on
stage

I'd have brought the house down
for sure

But I was always too far back from
the stage

A lonely little outcast for sure

I love the great tv show

The singing kettle news

There one week and gone the
next

it's a pity that we had to lose

I was really scared of the editor

Please bear in mind I was nine

I was not as brave as I would be
now

I'm sure now that he would be
kind

I hated the bit when you changed
the script

I wanted you to bring them back

The announcer was the worse
annoying type

I preferred the shouty Mr Spout
and Kettle back.

It wasn't the same without Mr
Spout and the big giant red kettle.
Even though they were scary.

Then came that day, that terrible
day

When you were no longer a band

I would have given you my ideas

For singing kettle news anyway.

I really want to meet the singing
kettle

I know they don't exist anymore

Artie, Cilla, Gary, Jane and the
others

And maybe peek in the editor's
door

I really want to meet the singing
kettle

I know they don't exist anymore

The tale of the ladybird.

 Ladybird flying in the garden.
One spot two spots half a dozen
spots.

Ladybird landing on a stone-cold
planter.

Tickles my fingers as she crawls
up my arm.

I am digging up weeds in the
garden.

Cleaning up Moria's garden

Ladybird is hungry and goes on
the bench.

Sniffs my chocolate sandwich and
M's egg salad sandwich.

Ladybird drinks the sweet. nectar
from the flowers.

Ladybird spots others just like her.
Spots and all.

Ladybird parties with a million others.

Written for Chris during a writing group

How did we meet?

We met on zoom in a room.

I was dancing on the moon.

I was scared so afraid

Wondering if it was true

Then we met on a street

And I felt like I would be with you
to eat.

First best friends then lovers

There will never be another.

I wrote this poem when I first met
Chris.

Chrissy

You fixed my heart when it was
badly broken

I thought I would always be only
reading Tolkien.

You put me back together.

I will love you forever.

Chrissy, you proved to me that
love is not just for teenagers.

Chrissy, I'm 33 and I don't care
that you are nearly forty.

Chrissy, I wish that we had met a
lot sooner.

Chrissy, I'll buy you a tie if you
promise to marry me.

Been looking for love all my life.

Now I want to be your wife.

I know that this sounds crazy.

But I'm ready to be your Lizzy.

I gave you all my heart.

Hope we'll never be apart.

I love you and you love me.

That's the way it's going to be

X34

Bus driver stops and opens the
door.

Of the wonderful incredible X34.

You can tell that they've been
mopping the floor.

As I step right into the X34

Take a seat and rest your feet.

Been doing some shopping in the
street.

It's freezing cold. Only glad that
the bus came.

It's snowing buckets. I just want
hame.

The town is white and full of
silence.

Snowflakes falling from the sky.

I'll fix my laces then I'm done.

To walk in this snow. I must try.

Bus driver, stop and open the
door.

Oh, wonderful incredible X34.

This is my stop I got to go out
there.

I'm only glad the bus driver cares.

I used the X34 for my shopping.

and going to work in kilwinning.

Then some mad men took my bus
away.

To make more money by the way.

Now I'm standing here with
frostbite.

The 25's nowhere in sight

I've been waiting an hour or
more.

I still miss the X34.

Bus driver please will you hurry
up now.

I'm frozen cold and tired and I
need a poo now.

I've been shopping in kilwinning.

And the cold rain is pouring.

I really miss the Days we had the
X34.

The 25 takes forever to open its
door.

In fact. it takes an hour to come.

And when it comes it is late all the
time.

Mad men took the X34 away.

The 25 is always late now by the
way.

I remember the days when we
used to say.

They'll never take the X34 away.

Please bring back the x34.

Written before joe became
president and Donald trump was
still in charge of USA.

Worse year ever.

Laptops breaking all the time.

Working from home for the
bosses brine.

Think the Tories plan to kill us all

But first they'll drive us up the
wall.

Donald trump is president joe

Will he stay or will he go

We won't know for a while

First, we'll have a little wine.

I never knew that I would live

To see the worst year ever Clive

Corona is not just a beer.

It's why we cannot laugh and
cheer

I hope that this is not the end

I really want to make a friend

I hope this plague don't kill us all.

With some stupid fool who
dropped the ball.

Go back to work one minute

Told to stay at home the next
minute.

What are we to do in England
now?

Glad I live in Scotland pal

The votes are being cast now

Who is picking up the call?

It's either Donald trump or joe

I hope they don't mess it all.

Now the votes are being counted.

Both teams are being hounded.

2020 feels like a bad dream

This year would make a Saint
scream

Will it be blue or red

The country is holding its breath.

2021 must be better

Can't cope with the terror

And the president is?

Tune in to our American station
to find out.

The door

Knock knock

Come in.

The flood.

As I watch the rising tide.

I feel so glad I'm still alive.

The river comes. Its suffocating.

The body of a child that's five.

So many people lost their homes.

Their livelihoods. Their
everything.

I see in the mud the rotten bones.

These people need help to start
again.

I wish I could make things right.

I wish I could fix this fright.

I wish this had never come.
The flood is flowing on and on.

Germany and Belgium flooded
too.

The flood it spreads so easily like
glue.

It makes me helpless to see them
suffer.

How can I help? What can I do?

Think the flood is heading to the
sea.

I wish we stopped burning fossil fuels.

Is this the way it's going to be?

Thousands lost in floods forever.

Series Nine by Elizabeth Mullen.

He was a hero. She was a zero. She was an outcast or so I've heard.

She was a lion. He was a donkey. He backed the wrong horse.

He was alone. She said the
words. That only a true fan
would say.

What the true fan had to say.
Haunts him to this very day.

That stupid fish thing totally
doesn't work.

Knightmare is so much better
pal.

That fish thing made no bloody
sense.

Knightmare should have had a
series nine.

He was so shocked. That she
could tell. They told her to
apologise.

So, she apologised for being
born. He was so torn. He gave
a gentle sigh.

She was alone. He told her.
Come and see my other shows.

Where she saw Knightmare
and now she REALLY knows.

Missed out first time around.

Now she loves that Knightmare
show.

Wishes she could break new
ground.

Like that man she used to
know.

Maybe there'll be a series nine.

Poor little yellowjacket

Poor little yellowjacket

I sense your fear and fright.

Poor little yellowjacket

Your coat looks smart and bright.

Poor little yellowjacket

Your sting cannot break through
the glass.

Poor little yellowjacket

I wonder if you are a boy or a girl

Poor little yellowjacket

I wish I could open the window

Poor little yellowjacket

I wish you were not down low

Poor little yellowjacket

I didn't see you leave the bus

Poor little yellowjacket

Your sting was in a rush

Poor little yellowjacket

Exhausted you lie on the window

Poor little yellowjacket

For you I carry a heart full of
sorrow.

Poor little yellowjacket

I wish I could have helped

Poor little yellowjacket

I was afraid that I would have
yelped.

Poor little yellowjacket

I was afraid of the sting

Poor little yellowjacket

You're pretty but I fear the sting

2020 BLUES

Well, I woke up one morning

 and I had the 2020 blues.

I bought myself a pair of trainers

because I had holes in my shoes.

The whole world's gone crazy

and I don't know what to do.

So, I bought a ukulele

to help me sing away the 2020
blues.

The thing came in kit form,

 So, I had to buy some pink paint
and glue.

I wanted to make my own ukulele

 So, looked on YouTube what to
do

The cats got their claws in

 and the dog started to sing too.

As I built my ukulele,

I sang away the 2020 blues.

The year's nearly over

and the end is nowhere in sight.

My dog jumped when I played the ukulele

for the very first time.

We've all had a bad year

Some got a terrible fright

Some of us lost folk

Some ran out of time

So please wear a mask

Not too much to ask

In memory of those

Who can't breathe through their
nose

And it's not funny

When folk sell you fake news

They say oh honey

Covid killed by dog chews

NOT

I wish that things

Would go back to normal

But this is life now

It's the new normal

So please wear a mask

And all wash your hands

I set you this task

Hope you understand

That was the 2020 blues

The 2020 blues.

Written for a boy I loved who
turned out to be like every other
man I met. Chris is different.

K

K the first time I saw your
handsome lovely face.

Was online at a zoom meeting
with folk from far away.

It doesn't matter to me that
you're from another place.

I feel that I just fell in love and
hope you'll find a way.

I feel very much I want to look
inside your pants.

I want to meet your mum and
dad, make friends with them of
course.

I'm trying to take it slow, but my
heart feels like its full of ants.

I really hope you love me and that
we'll last the course.

They say that true love will never
die.

I hope that I can spread my wings
and fly away with you.

I can't wait to hear our firstborn's
birth cry.

I know our love is full of joy and
I'm in love with you.

Written for a boy who I thought
loved me but didn't.

Miss unpopular 2021.

There was a time where I never
thought that anyone would ever
want me as a wife.

They call me fat and ugly and
suggest that I just make friends.

I never had a boyfriend or went to
a senior prom.

Voted little miss unpopular a
thousand times a year.

I thought I had a chance once, but
he turned to be gay.

Nobody ever fancies me. This is
how it goes.

I fancy someone, chat them up
and they never return the feelings
back.

The first kiss I had in college was
just two boys daring each other.

I was just happy to get a snog and
they didn't snog again. Yuck they
cried when they kissed me.

With you I thought you were
different but you're just the
bloody same.

You broke my heart. I trusted you.
I don't want to just be friends.

I trusted you in a way I have never
trusted before.

I was willing to have sex with you
and prove the bullies wrong.

I guess I'll always be miss
unpopular.

I'm never getting laid and the first
man to touch my naked body.

Will be cutting me up on a table
to find out how I died.

I am lonely now and I'm thinking
of become a nun.

Nun's get more of a sex life than I
do.

I'm a 34-year-old virgin soon and
that's how I will be remembered.

Here lies a girl who was
unpopular all her days.

Written for a boy I fancied who
didn't want me.

To my best hope at getting laid.

I wish I was a kleptomaniac
because then I would find it easy
to steal your heart.

I fancy you like sticky candy floss
in the hands of young girls.

I don't know how to do this. This
falling in love thing.

I'm told it is very easy. But I have
not got a clue.

I wish I was a scientist because I
want to look inside your brain.
Yes Mr. I do.

I want to know you inside and out
and that includes your pants.

I never felt like this before. I just
know I want more.

I know my insides feel funny and I
think I'm in love with you.

See the light

By Elizabeth Mullen

I hope that we don't suffer the
pain

Of defeat or failure again.

We are this close to making
history.

Let's hope it is not the same old
story.

Let's lift the trophy. It's not a
dream.

Let's avoid the dreaded
nightmare scream.

Let's do what folk said was
impossible.

You know that we are all able.

I am afraid to hope the impossible

I dream the impossible ever night.

I glare at teams who say you can't
do the impossible

I pray that Scotland will see the
light.

We are still waiting to break the
duck

At getting to the next round, we
are out of luck.

We never make it past the group
stage Bill

Next time I know we will.

I hope we get to face Spain.

And send them home to think
again.

Let's beat England and Germany

Let's beat them all. The teams are
many.

When we fall. We pick ourselves
up.

Next time this time for sure.

Humpty Dumpty's had a great fall.

So did Scotland they're off the
wall.

The tumble.

I was slowly making my way up
the stairs to my next class when
the girl pushed me. It wasn't an
accident. She viciously grabbed
my shoulder and before I could
say anything violently threw me
down the stairs. Just like I was a
piece of rubbish being tossed
aside.

I saw my life flash before me.

I lived through every single
taunting I have ever had thrown
at me. All in a spilt second.

My special needs teacher that
helps me in the classroom found

me at the foot of the stairs. I was lying on my back in shock and in pain.

"She pushed me down the stairs."

The teacher smiles. "It must have been an accident." She says in that sing song voice that treats me like a five-year-old.

"No" I answer. "She grabbed my shoulder and pushed me. "I show the teacher the violent move and the teacher looks puzzled.

"I said it was an accident." The girl says trying not to grin.

The teacher glares at me., "See it
was an accident. Now Elizabeth
you must apologize to Sally."

I bow my head and say sorry.

The teacher leaves. Sally laughs.

The attack

I opened my eyes.

He was there.

I saw him.

A grey and black shadow in the
darkness.

He came closer.

I tried to scream. I couldn't talk,
shout or scream. My throat was
frozen. I sat up.

He grabbed me.

I tried to push him away. He
grabbed my trousers and yanked
hard.

My fat belly saved me.

He yanked again. I tried to pull
them up and push him off me at
the same time.

He grabbed my hand. It was hairy.
His hands were like a gorilla. He
held something in his hands. I
kicked it off him. He grabbed my

foot. I touched his hands and pulled them off.

I thought he was going to kill me. Or worse. Rape me.

The light came on. I saw his blue top. I saw his dark brown hair and his grey eyes. I saw his shocked face.

He ran. I bravely gave chase. I couldn't find him. I went downstairs.

"Dad, do you know a man in a blue top."

"What?"

"There was a man in a blue top in my room. Do you know him?"

"Go back to sleep you were dreaming."

 "But he was real. "

 "I don't care If he was Father Christmas. Go back to bed. "

I signed and headed back up the stairs. My dad didn't believe me.

About half an hour later my dad was woken up by a clip clop sound. The sound repeated itself. Dad looked through the hatch to find out what I was doing when he saw a dark brown haired man in a black jacket creeping into the kitchen.

He was not dreaming. I was not
dreaming. That man was real.

Vase of flowers

I really really like a vase of flowers
on the window

It doesn't matter if they are real
or fake

As long as they are on the
window.

I have hayfever it's no mistake

Just place them at the window

You + me = CPR

Well, I'm sorry I had to slap your
face

But I wanted you still in the
human race

I got a fright when your lips
turned blue

I was thinking what else could I do

I could tell that you were dying on
me

So, I held your hand, had to make
them see

Half an hour I hid my fear

All the while thinking oh dear

And the only thing going through
my head was

You + me = CPR

I knew you only as pickle number
2

Might have fancied you but I
didn't let on

I feared they would say he's gone

That I would end up on the run

Your face was grey I thought
that's it

For the second time you got a
massive hit

I saved you out of love

I saved you out of kindness

My lovely blue eyed peaceful
dove

Wonder where you are now

Death of the queen

Goodnight ma'am
Sleep tight

Hope you see your man again

Waiting at the golden gate

A trip to Saltcoats beach.

The beach did not have a lot of
sand. The scared crab stood still.
The shark chased Sally and
another shark ate John. Simon
sidestepped to his left and stood
on a helpless squid. Harry
watched the strange scared crab
eat seaweed on the shore. Barry
went into a shop and bought
some sandwiches and crisps for
himself, Steve and Samuel.

Samuel had the last packet of salt
and vinegar crisps in the shop.
Steve had cheese and onion.
Barry did too.

Laura went seagull spotting and
saw one enter a shop and steal a
bottle of sprite. Laura drank the
cold sprite and the seagull pecked
her on the shin. Laura was then
grabbed by the angry shopkeeper.

Grace bought a stick of rock with
Saltcoats inside. Samuel did too.

Kerry saw the seagull eat the
sandwiches and salt and vinegar
crisps. It also pecked Samuel. The
seagull then stole the stick of rock
from both people.

Sally then got eaten by the shark.

Then the school bus came back to
the beach and the survivors went
home minus Sally, Laura and
John.

Laura went to jail for ten years.
The seagull is still there.

The Gatecrasher.

"I didn't mean to come here in
the first place. I got lost and I'm
meant to be in the other room."

"There's another convention?"

"No, it's a... Signing up for the radio thing."

"You are on the radio? Wow. Cough. Cough. I never met a radio presenter before."

"And I never met Pickle, or a guy dressed as him before, so we are even."

"Being on the radio sounds really cool."

"It is Pickle number two. It's amazing. Hey don't go to sleep on me. I need to keep you awake."

"I know. If I crash out with my heart beating the way it is, I might die. Cough. Cough."

"Pickle. I need you to stay with me. Pickle!" Elizabeth slaps the black-haired boy's face.

"Ouch. That hurt." Pickle groans.

"I know. But you nearly died on me."

"My heart is beating worse. I need to do special breathing." Pickle number two breathes deeply like a woman in labour.

"Is that the breathing that women in labour use."

"Yes. Funny enough."

"Let's role play labour and pretend you are having a baby. I'll help you with breathing."

"Ok." Pickle breathes deeply.

"Help will come soon. I hope."

"My friends will come. They have to."

Time past. Elizabeth wasn't sure how much time, but Pickle's face suddenly changed.

"I can see your mum. You look like her."

"You mean my gran right. My mum is still alive."

"Yeah, she's your gran. She looks
like you."

"Where is she?"

"She is behind you."

"I can't see her."

"She can see you."

"Hi gran."

"Holy Moses there's two of
them."

"Yeah, my gran was a twin."

"Her twin was stillborn."

"Yeah. How do you know that?"

"They told me."

"My gran died when I was nine."

I know. She told me."

"Pickle don't die."

I think it's my time to die. I don't want to go."

"What can I do to save you?"

"Pray for me. Pray for me to live."

"OK Pickle I will pray." Elizabeth lowers her head and prays.

"Pray harder."

"I pray that Pickle number 2 lives and recovers from this."

"You don't know me at all."

"I know I don't know him. But I care about him. I care about him very much. I don't want him to die."

"It's working. Thank you."

"I pray that Pickle number 2 will survive this issue with his heart and that his friends will come soon."

"It's still beating bad."

"Pickle please hold on. You are going to be alright. Your friends are coming. Spellcasting H. E. L. P."

"Try summoning him."

"How do you summon folk?"

"Say their name 3 times."

"Pickle number 1 Pickle number 1
Pickle number 1. Treguard
number 2 Treguard number 2
Treguard number 2. Treguard
number 1 Treguard number 1
Treguard number 1. Timmy
Timmy Timmy."

Half an hour later Elizabeth was
still calling for help with the same
pattern.

Pickle looks at Elizabeth. His face
is grey and pale. He looks bad.
Very bad. "I love you." He says
flickering his eyes.

"Pickle, I love you too. As a friend I mean." Pickle's eyes flicker and Elizabeth screams. "Pickle don't die."

Elizabeth slaps Pickle's face. It stops death but she can smell a strange smell like nail polish.

Elizabeth calls for help again using the summoning method.

Just then a hero walks in. It is Pickle from knightmare. Pickle gasps in shock and Elizabeth sees the danger.

"Pickle number 1 meet Pickle number 2. Pickle number 2 meet Pickle number 1. He's in labour."

"What" Pickle number one says shocked.

"He's got a heart condition."

"Ok."

"Listen I think Pickle's about to croak and believe me that is no joke. Just help me get his friends Treguard number 2. I don't care how you get him. Just hit him with the knapsack and knock some sense into him."

"I'll try."

"Please help. I need a hero, Pickle. Pickle number 2 needs a hero."

"Ok."

"Thank you."

Pickle number 2 was lying on the floor trying to breathe and stay calm."

Pickle number 1 leaves and heads over to the stage as Treguard number 2 shouts. "Pickle."

"Here I am master."

"What you are not my Pickle. Where is Pickle?"

"Where's the knapsack?"

"Over there." Treguard number 2 points backstage to a table.

"Ok master." Pickle leaps over and grabs the knapsack then hits

Treguard number 2 with it repeatedly.

 "Treguard number 1 help me knock some sense into your Pickle. He's hitting me with the knapsack." Treguard number 2 screamed.

"Pickle number 1" Treguard number 1 growled. "What are you doing? "

Pickle number 1 looked at Treguard and told him. "Pickle number 2 is dying back there. I don't feel well." He then collapsed on stage in front of the other audience members.

Treguard and a medic ran into the
stage.

 "It's not me that needs help but
Pickle number 2. "Pickle number 1
said getting up.

Treguard number 2 and Velma
the elf ran over to the red curtain.

Treguard 2 yelled "Push Pickle
Push."

"He can't Push the baby's stuck. "

 "What do you mean the baby's
stuck. "

 "Feel his pulse and you'll see
what I mean. "

The Black haired elf lady called
Velma felt Pickle number 2's
pulse. "Oh my god this baby really
is stuck. "

Treguard number 2 and Velma
scooped Pickle number 2 up and
carried him to the rucksack.

The rucksack held the drugs to
restart Pickle's heart.

 "Ok just giving you the first dose.
"

"it's not working. "

Ok second dose. "

The drugs kicked in.

"She saved my life. Elizabeth saved me. "

Treguard number 2 sighs a sigh of relief. Pickle number 2 is getting better from his heart issue.

"Why were you on your own with her? "

"The blond-haired lady Kate left us on our own. Kate was meant to stay with us. She went to the shop. She never came back. "

"She told me that you were ok. "

"She left me on my own. "

"She broke the golden rule. "

"Talk to Elizabeth. She saw her leave. I want Eizabeth here. "

Treguard number 2 picks up a rolled blue towel and places it on Pickle's chest. "There's your baby"

Pickle 2 laughs. Treguard number 2 leaves to find Elizabeth sobbing furiously in the chest of a nervous Pickle number 1.

"He's ok. "

"And the baby? "

"The baby's ok too."

"Is it a Boy or a girl. "

"it's a boy. "

"Can I see them. "

"Yeah, Pickle's asking for you! "

"The blonde-haired lady went to the shop. She never came back. "

"Did you want anything from the shop? "

"No. She shook her head at me as she asked. "

"Ok I'll talk to Kate. You sit with pickle and the baby you pretended he was having.

Kate was in trouble. Again.

Lucky the lamb.

The sheep cried out and Lucky
was born. He didn't start out
lucky. He needed the farmer's
help to breath. After learning to
breath his brother Larry was born.

Lucky and Larry were white
woolly sheep with black faces and
feet and Lucky had a white horse
shoe on his right cheek. Larry had
a pure black face and a white spot
on his left hind leg. These
markings made sure the farmer
did not mix them up.

As Lucky grew older, he loved
playing with Larry his brother and
all the other farm animals. There

was Charlie, Caleb, Christine, Carol, Clever, Pompom, Noisy, Spike, Nosy, Squawk, Cat and Claire the chicks. There was Clover, Lucy, Susan, Karen, Bob and Daisy the calves and Buttercup, Daffodil, Tulip and Rose the cows who always told the chicks and lambs to move it. He liked the little muddy pigs Percy, Penny, Pork, Chop, Peter, Paula, Lunchtime, Hungry, Suppertime, Breakfast and Paper.

One day Lucky heard a barking noise and saw a barking creature running towards the sheep. Bravely Lucky chased away the golden barking creature. "My

name is Dug the dog. I'm a
sheepdog." The puppy Dug
barked. Lucky asked. "What's a
sheepdog?" Dug explained that
he was meant to help the farmer
look after the sheep. Lucky soon
made friends with Dug. Larry
followed. Larry always followed
Lucky.

One day Lucky jumped out the
field and into the dirty road. A
green van drove by and some
disabled kids were going shopping
with the local youth club in Ayr.
The old man who was driving by
saw Lucky on the road and saw
the danger he was in. The old
man called Jack Tanner bravely

jumped out the car and chased
Lucky back into the field. Lucky
did not like being chased.

The others laughed at Lucky for
jumping out the field. But the
next day hustlers came to the
farm in a green muddy trailer. The
six hustlers wearing white overalls
and black boots with an old gas
mask on their faces started to
load the sheep into the trailer.
Lucky jumped the fence and ran
to the farmers House as fast as he
could. The farmer realising
something was wrong followed
Lucky. Lucky, Dug and Mr Brown
the farmer hurried and chased
the hustlers away. The sheep got

out the trailer and the hustlers were soon captured by police. The green trailer was taken away for testing and held as evidence.

Soon Lucky was bigger than his mum Sophie and stronger than his dad Ray. Lucky wasn't a lamb anymore. Ray the ram told his son about a wonderful place called market where he would find a wife and a new home. Soon Lucky, Larry and all of their friends went to market. Dug stayed behind.

At market they were sold as separate lots. First the young chickens, then the cows, then the bull, then the pigs, then the lambs. Larry was sold then it was Lucky's turn.

Lucky struggled to pull free but relaxed when he heard his brother had been brought by the same guy who now owned him.

Lucky was still scared what if he was going to be eaten. He knew some were eaten and some were not. Lucky was forced into a trailer and driven far away to his new home.

When he got there to the farm in Beith, he was amazed that he had been bought as a mascot by the local farm museum in Ayrshire.

His brother and all his old friends
were there. Except Dug of course.
But Dug had not left the farm
with them that day. Dug had his
own job to do at Lucky's old
home.

There were lots of new folk too.
Stephanie the young sheep and
her sister Sally. Laura the llama,
Grace and Nibbles the goats and
Gary and Ginny the Guinea pigs.
Peck and Poke the geese and
Swimmer and Diver the ducks. As
well as Dominic and Daniel the
old dogs.

It was a working farm that made
ice cream and cheese. It kept the

animals alive, and they lived happy lives here.

Lucky and Stephanie got together, and Larry and Sally paired up as well and soon there were babies on the farm. There were twin lambs for each of the sheep, several litters of piglets and a dozen calves. There were also lots of baby chickens, some baby ducks and a few baby geese. There was a baby male goat called Buttalot and a litter of Guinea pigs.

The farm became famous for its ice cream and cheese and the animals were all happy. And one

of Dug's puppies found her way to
the famous farm. Her name was
Missie. She was a sheepdog too
and she found some buried
treasure in the field one day. But
that is another story to be told.

The end.

The Christmas tree angel.

There was once a Christmas tree
angel who was sitting on a shelf in
the local charity shop all sad and
alone. She wanted to see her first
Christmas as part of a family.
Soon a young family came into

the shop. They see her and were
amazed at her beauty. They
picked her up and took her to the
checkout and bought her.

The next day it was Christmas eve
and there put her onto the tree
that they had. The Christmas tree
angel was incredibly happy and
was glad that she had new friends
that would help the Christmas
tree angel if she needed it.

The next day the Christmas tree
angel watched the kids open their
gifts from Santa and there was an
extra gift at the end for the angel.

It was a little friend for the angel.
A tiny robin.

They put the robin on the tree
and the angel was never sad or
alone again.

The end.

The Leprechaun's Gold.

Once upon a time there was a
three foot high leprechaun all
dressed in green called Lorcan
McChest. He had a huge black pot
of shiny gold that he hid in an
excessively big tree.

One day a naughty robber called
Sean McDog heard about the
leprechaun's gold and came to the

large tree carrying a spade and started digging. He dug and he dug until he had dug up the huge pot of gold. He then took the huge and heavy pot of gold away.

The leprechaun was incredibly angry when he found his pot of gold was missing. He knew he couldn't find the scoundrel on his own so he went to the local police station in his native country of Ireland to see if they could help.

When the young trainee police officer Paddy McGuinness saw the leprechaun come into the police station, he couldn't help but laugh at the three foot tall poor hapless leprechaun. Luckily, his boss knew something was up.

"What's happened here?" The police officer asked. "Did someone steal your gold Lorcan?"

Lorcan nodded. "Someone went and stole my pot of gold and I need it back."

The police offered to search the neighbourhood for it.

Meanwhile the robber Sean McDog was looking for a pawn shop for his ill-gotten gold. The pawn shops knew it was leprechaun gold by the mark of the shamrock on the gold. They all refused to take it.

Suddenly the leprechaun smelled his gold and followed the scent.

He found Sean McDog carrying
the heavy pot of gold and looking
about for somewhere to hide it.
The leprechaun caught Sean and
told him. "That's my gold, give it
back and I'll give you three
wishes."

Sean handed the pot over and said
cheekily. I wish for lots of gold, I
wish to be famous, and I wish I
didn't need to steal things to earn
money.

The leprechaun granted his three
wishes with a laugh.

Suddenly Sean found he could
poop gold. Tons of it.

The leprechaun tried to take his
gold back. Sean wouldn't let him.

The leprechaun got angry and
made Sean's gold inside him
double the rate of production
inside his bowel. Sean became
extremely uncomfortable.

The leprechaun took his gold back
and Sean hurried to the hospital.

A passing police car saw Sean and
arrested him. There in a cell Sean
became famous for pooping tons
of gold an hour. He went to
hospital and became world famous
as the man who could poop gold
and soon found a new job as a
bank teller. Sean never stole from
anyone ever again. He knew he

would be caught if he tried to.
Sean just couldn't tell when the
next batch of gold would appear.
Gold always appeared when he
was working on something.

Meanwhile the leprechaun put his
gold at the end of a rainbow. It
was safer there. Not many humans
could get to the end of a rainbow.
Many had tried. Almost all had
failed.

The Valentine's Day Surprise.

David Clown dressed in a fancy
black and white suit and tie was
pacing up and down the fancy

restaurant holding a small box in his hand. He was looking at the other couples sitting at the tables and waiting for his girlfriend Jenny Brown. They were booked in for a meal at 7:30 pm.

It was now 7:29 pm. The date was the 14th of February 2021. Valentine's day.

The fat faced ugly Jenny Brown with the huge waist, chest and bum swam into the room in her size 30 dress.

David looked at how beautiful she was. Her piles of fat filled flesh draped over her bones and made her look like a hippo. She was ugly in heart, and she had the looks to match.

David was not good looking either. He had a goblin face as well as an ugly heart too. They both hated disabled folk. They saw them as beneath them. Jenny's heart was cold like stone just like his. That was why he had bullied a red haired short fat but lots thinner than Jenny was wee disabled lassie called Elaine Morgan. He knew Jenny felt the same way about red haired short people that were disabled. She had bullied Elaine as well. Elaine was born disabled and had been very smart at school. She was his best victim.

"Let's get to the table and have a seat." Jenny yelled loudly disturbing David's thoughts about his glory days at school. "I'm starving."

David took Jenny's hand and took her to the table as the server watched the two love birds dancing across the room. "I'm paying. What would you like to eat Darling?" He asked feeling happy and hungry for food and a good time later.

"I'll have the Valentine's Day Surprise and I want it right now."

Jenny yelled loudly. "I hope that freak of a waitress doesn't come to us." She snarled at the red haired brown eyed autistic server.

The autistic server came over. She was doing her job by serving these people as the other waiters were busy. She hoped they would not give her any grief. She had bills to pay, a man that loved her deeply and family to feed.

"Two Valentine's Day Surprises please you little freak." David yelled at the red haired short clumsy autistic server as she took their order."

"And the free bottle of wine spaz." Shouted Jenny as the poor server tried to keep her balance while carrying a tray full of heavy plates.

She seemed familiar to them. Surely this was not the same stupid autistic kid they both knew at school. Gated Academy had been a wonderful place they could bully all they wanted, and the teachers would let them. She was their sweetest victim. So sweet she couldn't even fight back, and she had been blamed for bullying him. It was a joke right. David Clown the cruellest bully of them all bullied by an innocent sweet girl. She didn't know how to fight back. She couldn't even walk properly.

He wondered if she had passed her exams then decided she had failed them all. She was dumb. Thick and dumb. That's what David believed. David was wrong to believe that.

Jenny started talking to David and held his hand. "The meal is here."

They then feasted on the hot posh mushroom soup that was blended into a cream and mixed with a pale milk juice that was creamy and tasted divine. They then had mushrooms with their steak and chips and laughed cruelly at the obviously autistic server as she dropped a fork and bent over to pick it up.

They shouted all the slurs to do with disability they could think of. Mongrel was only one of the words they said. She wisely ignored them. She had heard it all before from them.

Suddenly David leaned over to Jenny. "There's something I have to tell you." There was a box in his hand.

Jenny leaned in closer. "What is it honey bun?"

David handed over a small box to Jennifer. "My stomach hurts. Think I laughed too much at that autistic server." David said holding his stomach.

"Yeah, my stomach hurts too. I don't feel well." Jenny moaned before vomiting her guts all over David Clown.

David seen and smelled the vomit, and he began to vomit all over Jenny.

The server who had passed all her many exams at school and was the same youth that they had bullied at school came over. "Is everything ok?" She asked the vomiting couple as they vomited up blood on each other.

Getting no response, she told her boss to phone an ambulance for David Clown and Jenny Brown as they had been suddenly taken ill at their table.

David and Jenny's hearts were beating extremely fast now. Was it love, passion or poison. They didn't know and were too ill to care now. They fainted in their vomit filled dinner as the ambulance came.

Her boss Steve Throne hid the jar of Chinese herbs in the bin. There was no point in keeping the jar.

He would only go to prison for life for his cousin Elaine Morgan if it were found that he had poisoned them. Revenge was a dish best served with mushrooms and a Chinese jar full of aconite. Elaine didn't know that they had been poisoned. Steve hadn't told her.

David Clown and Jenny Brown would never bully anyone ever again.

In fact, they would never do much of anything again. That included breathing.

The day the queen died.

On a date

It went great

Had gammon steak and chips with
pineapple.

Chris is tasty just like an apple.

Had sticky toffee pudding

And it was filling

Got the bus

Was in a rush

Called Judy on the phone

On my mobile phone

Got home at four

Went through the door

Found out the queen was very ill.

So much so they'd sent for
Charles and will.

Newsreaders dressed in black and
white.

Something wrong not right.

Put on a black dress cause things
felt odd

Drank some coke and the news
was odd

Went in my room.

No meeting on zoom.

Next thing the queen has died.

When the queen died.

Everyone cried.

That's what happened the day the
queen died.

Long live...

Long live the queen

Long live the king

Long live the prince

Long live the princess

The queen is dead

The king is dead

Long live the king

August

A baby is born

Unique and brave

Good and noble

Unicorn pure

Special little baby

This is my birth month

August

Disco

Everybody in the house say boo

Bbbbbboooooooooooooooo

Aaaaaaaaaaaaaaaaaaahhhhhhhh

October

Over the hills the kids go

Catching the leaves to dress up in

The witching day will soon begin

Oi ho who nicked my pumpkin

Bats and cats stalk the windows

Everyone is dressing up

Ryan wins as a crow.

October.

Cold

My dose is docked I can't smell, I
can't eat. Oh better now.

Smells

I smell the leaves on the ground

The crispy smell and bright
colours

I smell the smell of burning wood

The children singing in the dark

I smell the summer breeze

The seagulls swoop on my fish
and chips

I smell the frying fish and chips

As I try and get some lunch.
Again.

I smell my dad's aftershave on the
face of my love

My wedding has all my family. Yes
dad is there.

I smell the sweet smell of my
newborn firstborn son.

His skin is soft and smooth and I
love to cuddle him.

I smell the roses growing on my
dad's tidy grave.

We buried him with my mum on
Easter Sunday.

I smell the burning fireplace as we
cuddle up together

It's funny how smells bring you
back to past memories.

Largs

I feel warm and the breeze is cool

I smell the salty water and the cooking food

I see the seagulls begging for scraps

I hear the children playing and the dogs barking

I taste the delicious fish and chips.

I lick the freezing ice cream that is melting

I feel the touch of a warm friendly dog.

It was a great day in largs.

The Artist

Painting for sale

Who wants to buy a painting?

A unique one of a kind Painting.

Place a bid or buy it now

Sold but for a tiny sum.

Worth millions after death

Worth Pennies in life

My naughty uncle William

My naughty uncle william has
been very very bad.

He drunk and drove and crashed
his car and now its getting toad.
How sad.

The policemen came and got him
and put him in the nick.

He needs a smacked bottom and
a tiny little kick.

It's going to be a fine and a ban as
well I think.

Knowing him, he'll make it worse
and get years in the nick.

We've got to take the cats as he
will turn to drink.

And wreck the place and smash it
all. Even the kitchen sink.

Teenage gatecrasher

Her name is Lizzie

She has a dream you see

She's very busy

She wants to fit in you see

She walks through the door

And sees something more.

She doesn't know who you are

Will you give a dam about her?

She's just a teenage, gatecrasher

She's just a teenage, gatecrasher

She's never seen knightmare

So, how can this girl fit in here?

She sees a man

He set up a master plan

He's very calm

She tells him where the plan went wrong

He says will you be long?

She goes on and on

He knows he's a donkey

The message is understood wonky

Woah

Oh yeah, outcast, she's nothing
but a zero

What must she do to become a
legendary hero

She meets a boy

He's older, so not a toyboy

He has a wonky heart

She doesn't want to be apart

His name is pickle

He gets in a pickle

She figures out what to do

She saves his life as his lips turn
blue

I heard you saved our friend and
we are grateful, young hero.

To show that you fit in, we'll play
with you. We'll play knightmare.

You are no longer a hated zero,
Young hero.

We'll show what you missed. Too
young to see knightmare.

Oh yeah, it's true.

I was the girl who saved him,
Became a hero.

His lips turned blue.

I was the zero who became a
legendary, hero.

Not just a teenage, gatecrasher

Not just a teenage, gatecrasher

She's now a legendary, hero

No longer a legendary, zero.

From legends, heroes are made.

Land of timorous beasties.

The drummers are drumming,
and the pipers are piping

The tartan is colourful and has
many designs.

The weather is roasting, and the
thistles need watering

So, lift your kilt and water the
thistles.

This is the land of timorous
beasties

And of whiskey, Irn bru and
haggis.

And in Scotland we have the
unicorn

Drinking pints with the Scottish
lion

We must wave the saltire for our
Scottish pride

Cheer on our folks as they take all
the gold.

Just being young and Scottish is a
very bumpy ride.

We are cheeky even when we are
old.

I think there's been a murder and
someone's been kilt

Oh it's just tomato ketchup
there's been nae murder here.

500 Scottish pounds just to clean
my bogging kilt

The dry cleaners are being
bleeding bold.

The unicorn is dancing in his
green tartan kilt

The lion is doing an amazing
highland fling

He's lifting the unicorn over his
shoulder

And the unicorn is playing with his
ding a ling

The lion roars on. The lion roars
on.

The unicorn purrs and lifts his tail

The lion roars on. The lion roars
on.

The unicorn purrs and lifts his tail.

And we forgot to add nessie from
loch ness

So to nessie we all hail. Hail
nessie!

The end of the book.

Hope you enjoyed it.

If not don't cry.

I really hope I left you

With a tear in each eye.